country. He attacked and exposed its enemies and betrayers with a boldness and integrity, which must endear his memory to every true and sincere patriot.

In presenting Aristophanes, therefore, to your Lordship, we present him to one, whom he, had he been an Englishman, would have chosen for his patron. Permit us, therefore, to make him this amends for the injury done him in our translation, and to subscribe ourselves,

My LORD, Your Lordship's most Obedient, and most Humble Servants,
HENRY FIELDING, WILLIAM YOUNG.

DRAMATIS PERSONÆ
MEN
Plutus, the God of Riches
Chremylus, An Old Yeoman in decayed circumstances
Blepsidemus, An Old Yeoman in decayed circumstances
Dicæus, a just and honest Man
Sycophantes, a Sycophant, or common Informer
Neaniscus, a young Gallant
Mercury
Priest of Jupiter
Cario, a Slave belonging to Chremylus
Chorus of Yeomen
WOMEN
The Wife of Chremylus
An Old Woman

SCENE: Athens

ACT I

SCENE I

Scene, the street in Athens before the house of Chremylus. **CARIO** and **CHREMYLUS** following **PLUTUS**.

CARIO
O Jupiter, and all ye Gods! what a vexatious thing it is to be the slave of a mad master! for, be the servant's advice never so excellent, if his master takes it into his head not to follow it, the poor domestic is by necessity forced to partake all the bad consequences. Fortune permits not the natural lord to have any power over his own person; but transfers it all to the purchaser. Well! these things are all so. However, I do complain (and my complaint is just) of that oblique deity, who sings forth his oracles from his golden tripod. Who, though he is both a physician and a prophet, a very good one too, as folks say, hath sent my master away in such a fit of the spleen, that with his eyes open he follows behind a blind fellow. Doing thus, the very reverse of what is agreeable to reason: for, whereas the blind are always led

by us who can see, this master of mine follows the guidance of the blind; nay, and compels me also to do the same: and all this without the blind rascal's answering us a single word. There is, therefore, no reason why I should be silent any longer; unless you will tell me, Sir, for what purpose we follow this fellow, I shall be very troublesome, indeed I shall—I know you will not lift your hand against a man with a sacred chaplet on his head.

CHREMYLUS
By Jupiter! if you plague me, I will,—first taking off your chaplet, to punish you the more.

CARIO
This is trifling: I shall never leave off till you tell me who that fellow there is. It is my great affection to you, which makes me so extremely vehemently inquisitive.

CHREMYLUS
Well: I will not hide it from thee; for, of all my domestics, I believe thee to be the most faithful, and most expert at concealing what thou canst of thy master's! Thou knowest, that I a religious and upright man as I am, have had very ill success in the world—nay, have suffered extreme poverty.

CARIO
Ay, Ay, I know it very well.

CHREMYLUS
Whilst others have acquired great riches, being at the same time guilty of sacrilege, public incendiaries, informers, and villains of all kinds.

CARIO
I am persuaded of it.

CHREMYLUS
I went therefore to consult Apollo, concluding indeed the quiver of my miserable days to be almost shot out, to inquire of him, for the sake of my son, , who is my only child, whether it was his interest to depart from his father's morals, and to become crafty, unjust, entirely corrupt; for these seemed to me the necessary qualifications for this world.

CARIO
What, from his garlands, chatter'd forth the God?

CHREMYLUS
You shall hear. The god told me this plainly: The first person whom I should meet after I departed from the temple, him he commanded me never to quit, till I had prevailed on him to accompany me to my house.

CARIO
And pray who was the first person you met?

CHREMYLUS
Why, this very person here before us.

Plutus by Henry Fielding & William Young

Henry Fielding was born at Sharpham Park, near Glastonbury, in Somerset on April 22nd 1707. His early years were spent on his parents' farm in Dorset before being educated at Eton.

An early romance ended disastrously and with it his removal to London and the beginnings of a glittering literary career; he published his first play, at age 21, in 1728.

He was prolific, sometimes writing six plays a year, but he did like to poke fun at the authorities. His plays were thought to be the final straw for the authorities in their attempts to bring in a new law. In 1737 The Theatrical Licensing Act was passed. At a stroke political satire was almost impossible. Fielding was rendered mute. Any playwright who was viewed with suspicion by the Government now found an audience difficult to find and therefore Theatre owners now toed the Government line.

Fielding was practical with the circumstances and ironically stopped writing to once again take up his career in the practice of law and became a barrister after studying at Middle Temple. By this time he had married Charlotte Craddock, his first wife, and they would go on to have five children. Charlotte died in 1744 but was immortalised as the heroine in both Tom Jones and Amelia.

Fielding was put out by the success of Samuel Richardson's Pamela, or Virtue Rewarded. His reaction was to spur him into writing a novel. In 1741 his first novel was published; the successful Shamela, an anonymous parody of Richardson's novel.

Undoubtedly the masterpiece of Fielding's career was the novel Tom Jones, published in 1749. It is a wonderfully and carefully constructed picaresque novel following the convoluted and hilarious tale of how a foundling came into a fortune.

Fielding was a consistent anti-Jacobite and a keen supporter of the Church of England. This led to him now being richly rewarded with the position of London's Chief Magistrate. Fielding continued to write and his career both literary and professional continued to climb.

In 1749 he joined with his younger half-brother John, to help found what was the nascent forerunner to a London police force, the Bow Street Runners. Fielding's ardent commitment to the cause of justice in the 1750s unfortunately coincided with a rapid deterioration in his health. Such was his decline that in the summer of 1754 he travelled, with Mary and his daughter, to Portugal in search of a cure. Gout, asthma, dropsy and other afflictions forced him to use crutches. His health continued to fail alarmingly.

Henry Fielding died in Lisbon two months later on October 8th, 1754.

Index of Contents

DEDICATION

TO THE RIGHT HONORABLE THE LORD TALBOT

My Lord,
In an age when learning hath so few friends, and fewer patrons, it might require an apology to introduce an ancient Greek poet to a person of an exalted station. For could the poet himself revive, and attend many such in his own person, he would be esteemed an unfashionable visitor, and might, perhaps, find some difficulty in gaining admittance.

But when we reflect on the revered name of the late Lord Chancellor of Great Britain, who, at the head of the greatest excellences and abilities, which ever warmed the heart, or embellished the understanding of man, preserved (which is, perhaps, the highest of human perfections) the most tender regard for the distressed; when we recollect what manifest tokens you have given that you inherit the virtues of that truly great and amiable person, we are emboldened, rather than discouraged, by this very consideration, to address the following attempt to your Lordship.

Permit us then, my Lord, to recommend Aristophanes; and with him, the distressed, and at present, declining, state of learning to your protection.

The greatness of this author's genius need not be mentioned to your Lordship; but there is a much stronger recommendation to one of your known principles. He exerted that genius in the service of his

CARIO

And can you be so dull to misapprehend the god's meaning, which declares to you in the plainest manner, that your son should pursue the manners of his country.

CHREMYLUS

Whence do you infer this?

CARIO

Most certainly. A blind man may see into this oracle, that it is extremely advantageous to exercise all kind of corruption at this present season.

CHREMYLUS

The oracle can by no means lean to this; it tends to something more important. And if this fellow will but tell us, who he is, and for what purpose, or on what occasion, he is come hither with us, we may then understand what our oracle means.

CARIO [To **PLUTUS**]

Come on; you, Sir, first and foremost, tell us who you are, or consequences will follow.

[Laying his stick on **PLUTUS'S** shoulder.

CHREMYLUS

It behoves you to speak to him immediately.

SCENE II

PLUTUS, **CARIO**, CHREMYLUS.

PLUTUS

I then desire much grief may attend thee.

CARIO

Do you understand, Sir, whom he declares himself to be?

CHREMYLUS

It is to you, not me he speaks thus: for you questioned the gentleman in an awkward and rude manner. [To **PLUTUS**]
But, Sir, if you delight in the behaviour of a gentleman, declare yourself to me.

PLUTUS

I then declare, I wish much wailing may attend thee.

CARIO

The gentleman, and the omen, Sir, are both your own.

CHREMYLUS

By Ceres, no joy shall ever attend thee: for, if thou dost not unfold thyself, to a miserable end will I bring thee, thou miserable wretch.

PLUTUS
Good gentlemen, depart from me, I beseech you.

CHREMYLUS
No, by no means.

CARIO
Odso! Master, I will tell you the best method in the world to deal with him. I will put this fellow to the most execrable end imaginable: for, having led him up to the top of some precipice, there leaving him, away go I—that tumbling from thence, the gentleman—may break his neck.

CHREMYLUS
Away with him then immediately.

[**CARIO** lays hold on **PLUTUS**.

PLUTUS
O by no means!

CHREMYLUS
Will you not tell then?

PLUTUS
Ay, but if you should know who I am, I am certain, you will still do me some mischief, and not dismiss me.

CHREMYLUS
Not we, by all the gods, if you will but—

PLUTUS
Take your hands off from me.

CARIO
There, you are at your liberty.

PLUTUS
Hear me then: for, it seems I must discover what I had so firmly resolved to conceal. Know then that I am Plutus.

CHREMYLUS
O thou most accursed of all mortals. What! Art thou Plutus, and would'st thou conceal thyself?

CARIO
What! you, Plutus? in such a miserable pickle—O Phoebus, Apollo, and O ye Gods! and O ye Dæmons, and O Jupiter!—How say you? And art thou he indeed?

PLUTUS

Indeed.

CHREMYLUS

What! he himself.

PLUTUS

The very self-same he.

CHREMYLUS

Tell me then, whence comes it that thou art in this dirty condition?

PLUTUS

I come, Sir, from the house of one Patroclus, who hath never been at the expense of washing himself, from his mother's womb.

CHREMYLUS

But pray tell me, how came you by this misfortune in your eyes?

PLUTUS

Jupiter, out of envy to mankind, afflicted me thus: for, when I was a little boy, I threatened, that I would only visit the just, and the wise, and the modest among them; whereupon he struck me with blindness, that I might not distinguish those from others. To such a degree doth this good envy good men!

CHREMYLUS

And yet it is by the good and just only that he is honored.

PLUTUS

I agree with you.

CHREMYLUS

Well, Sir, and if you should be restored to your sight, would you now avoid the habitations of the wicked?

PLUTUS

I do promise it.

CHREMYLUS

And you would frequent the just?

PLUTUS

Most certainly: for it is a long while since I have seen them.

CHREMYLUS

No wonder, truly: for neither have I, who have my eyes, seen any such lately.

PLUTUS

Well: now dismiss me; since you know every thing concerning me.

CHREMYLUS
No, by Jupiter, we will stick so much the closer to you.

PLUTUS
Did I not say you would be troublesome to me?

CHREMYLUS
Be prevailed on, I beseech you, and forsake me not: for, should you seek him never so diligently, you will not find an honester man. No, by Jupiter, will you not; for, indeed, there is no other honest man besides myself.

PLUTUS
Ay, all of you say this: but when once you have possession of me, and are become rich, you throw off the mask, and grow rampant in iniquity.

CHREMYLUS
It is indeed too commonly so: yet all men are not villains.

PLUTUS
Yes, by Jove, every mother's son of you.

CARIO [Aside]
You shall roar aloud for this, Sir.

CHREMYLUS
That you may know then how many advantages you will enjoy under my roof, only lend me your attention, and I will make you sensible. I flatter myself, indeed, I flatter myself, (with the assistance of Heaven be it spoken) that I shall deliver you from this infirmity of your eyes, and restore you to perfect sight.

PLUTUS
Indeed you shall not: for I have no desire to see any more.

CARIO
What doth the fellow say? This is a miserable dog in his own nature.

PLUTUS
Should Jupiter, who so well knows the follies of mankind, hear I had recovered my sight, he would pound me in a mortar.

CHREMYLUS
Doth he less to you now, who suffers you to stroll about stumbling in this manner?

PLUTUS
I know not what he may do: but I dread him exceedingly.

CHREMYLUS

Indeed, thou art the greatest coward of all deities. Do you think the power of Jupiter, and all his thunderbolts, would be of a triobolus consequence to you, if you could once recover your sight, though it were for never so little time.

PLUTUS

O miserable wretch! utter not such things.

CHREMYLUS

Be under no concern: for I will demonstrate that your power is much greater than that of Jupiter.

PLUTUS

You demonstrate this of me!

CHREMYLUS

Yes, by heavens! Instantly will I. By whose means doth Jupiter reign over the gods?

CARIO

By the means of money: for he hath the most of it.

CHREMYLUS

Well, and who furnishes him with these means?

CARIO

This honest gentleman here.

CHREMYLUS

And through whom do men sacrifice to Jupiter—Is it not through him there?

CARIO

Ay, by Jupiter, for they pray aloud for riches.

CHREMYLUS

Most certainly he is the cause, and if he pleased, could easily put an end to their sacrifices.

PLUTUS

How so, pray?

CHREMYLUS

Because no man could offer an ox, nor even a barley-cake, no, nor any other thing, without your good pleasure.

PLUTUS

How!

CHREMYLUS

How! Why he will not know how to purchase any thing, unless you are present, and give him the money: so that if the power of Jupiter be offensive to you, you alone will be able to demolish it.

PLUTUS

How say you? Do men sacrifice to him through me?

CHREMYLUS

I do say so. And by Jupiter! if there is any thing splendid, or beautiful, or lovely, among men, it proceeds from you; for to money all things pay obedience.

CARIO

Even I myself, for a small piece of money, am become a slave: because I was not so rich as some people.

CHREMYLUS

They say too of the Corinthian courtesans, that, if a poor lover attacks them, they will not even lend him an ear: but when a rich lover presents himself before them, they will themselves present any thing to him.

CARIO

They say that boys will present too: not for the sake of their lovers, but of money.

CHREMYLUS

You speak of prostitutes, not the worthier sort: for those never ask for money.

CARIO

Why, what do these ask for?

CHREMYLUS

One will accept a fine horse, another a pack of hounds.

CARIO

O then it is probable they are ashamed to ask for the money: they are pleased to cover their iniquity with the name of a present.

CHREMYLUS

All arts, all crafts known amongst mankind, are invented through thee. One sits down, and cuts out leather; another hammers out brass, a third hammers up wainscot, and a fourth casts the gold he hath recèived from thee. This filches away clothes from the public bagnio, another breaks open houses. One cleans cloth, another skins, another tans them; one deals in onions: nay, through thee, that gallant, when surprised with another man's wife, is stripped as naked as when he was born.

PLUTUS

Unhappy wretch that I am! I never knew a syllable of all this before.

CHREMYLUS [To **CARIO**]

Doth not the mighty emperor of Persia owe all his splendor to this person?

CARIO

Are not all public assemblies called together through him?

CHREMYLUS

What! dost not thou man our gallies? answer me.

CARIO

Doth not he maintain the foreign troops in Corinth?

CHREMYLUS

Will not Pamphilus owe many a groan to thee?

CARIO

And will not Belonopoles together with Pamphilus?

CHREMYLUS

Is it not through him that we support the F—ts of Argyrius?

CARIO

Ay, Sir, and is it not through him that we support the stories of Philepsius?

CHREMYLUS

Do we not through thee send auxiliaries to the Egyptians?

CARIO

Is not Nais through thee enamored of Philonides?

CHREMYLUS

Nay, the tower of Timotheus.—

CARIO

O may it fall on thy head.

CHREMYLUS

Are not all matters, in short, transacted through thee? For thou art the whole and sole author of all things, whether evil or good—Assure yourself, Sir, you are.

CARIO

This I am sure of—that in all battles they obtain the victory, into whose scale this gentleman throws himself.

PLUTUS

What I! who am but one; can I effect such mighty matters?

CHREMYLUS

Can you! Ay, by Jupiter, and many more too: for no man ever had his fill of thee; of all other things we may be surfeited: even with love.

CARIO

With bread.

CHREMYLUS
With poetry.

CARIO
With sweetmeats.

CHREMYLUS
With honor.

CARIO
With cheese-cakes.

CHREMYLUS
With bravery.

CARIO
With figs.

CHREMYLUS
With glory.

CARIO
With hasty-pudding.

CHREMYLUS
With the command of armies.

CARIO
With pease-porridge.

CHREMYLUS
Whereas of thee none ever had his fill: For when any one hath acquired thirteen talents, he becomes the more desirous of acquiring sixteen; and when he hath compassed these, he then desires forty; and if he fails in his last wish, he complains he hath none of the comforts of life.

PLUTUS
You seem to me to speak very well; I apprehend only one thing.

CHREMYLUS
Tell me what.

PLUTUS
How I shall be able to retain the possession of this power, which you represent me to have.

CHREMYLUS
By Jove, you need not fear it: but indeed, all men agree that thou art a most timorous animal.

PLUTUS

Not in the least. This is no more than the scandal of a housebreaker, who, when he had stolen into a house, and found every thing so cautiously locked up, that he was able to carry off no booty; he, forsooth, called my prudence timidity.

CHREMYLUS
However, be under no concern now: for, if you will but heartily enter into my proposals, I will undertake to make you more quick-sighted than Lynceus himself.

PLUTUS
But how will you be able to effect this, being but a mortal?

CHREMYLUS
I have very good hopes from what Apollo himself, shaking his Pythian laurel, communicated to me.

PLUTUS
Is he then privy to this?

CHREMYLUS
He is, I assure you.

PLUTUS
Be very cautious.

CHREMYLUS
Good Sir, give yourself no trouble about it: for, be assured, tho' at the expense of my life, I will accomplish it.

CARIO
And I promise you too, if you desire it.

CHREMYLUS
And many others will assist us, who are so honest, that they now want bread.

PLUTUS
Alas! you promise me very sorry assistants.

CHREMYLUS
Not at all, provided you change their circumstances, and make them rich: but, Cario, do thou run away with the utmost expedition.

CARIO
You will please to tell me what I am to do.

CHREMYLUS
Call hither my brother-farmers—you will find them, probably, in the fields sweating at their hard labor—bid them come hither, that every one may have his share in this Plutus.

CARIO

Well, I am going: but let some of your family within take care of this beef-steak here.

CHREMYLUS
That shall be my care—But away, fly instantly—And now, Plutus, thou most excellent of all deities, be pleased to go in with me; for this is the house, which you must this day fill with riches, by all methods whatsoever.

PLUTUS
Oh! Sir, I swear to you, I never enter another man's house without the utmost concern; for I have never been dealt well with in any. If I enter the house of a miser, he instantly buries me deep under ground; and if a worthy friend comes to ask him for a little piece of money, he denies me stoutly, says that he never saw me: but, if I visit a mad-headed fellow, I am exposed to whores and dice, and in a moment turned naked out of doors.

CHREMYLUS
But you have never lighted on a moderate man before: for my part, this was ever my way. I rejoice in frugality more than any man alive; and so I do in expense, whenever it is necessary to be expensive. But let us go in: for I am desirous that you should see my wife, and my only son, whom I love dearer than any thing—I mean, after you.

PLUTUS
I verily believe you.

CHREMYLUS
For why should any man tell a falsehood to you?

ACT II

SCENE I

Scene, the open country.

CARIO, CHORUS.

CARIO
O yes! All you that live upon grass-sallets, as well as my master, my good friends, and countrymen, and lovers of hard work; come, hasten, hurry, the time admits no delay; it is, indeed, the very nick of time, when your assistance is required.

CHORUS
You perceive we have been long bustling towards you with all our might, making the best haste in the power of feeble old men: but you would have me run as fast as yourself—besides, first tell me on what account your master hath sent for us.

CARIO
I have been telling you a long time: but you don't hear me. My master then says, that he will deliver you

from that cold and comfortless life you now lead, and make you all live pleasantly.

CHORUS
What is all this? Whence doth this fellow talk in such a manner?

CARIO
Why, my good pains-taking men, he hath brought home with him a certain old gentleman, who is all dirty, crooked, wretched, wrinkled, bald, toothless—Nay, and by Jupiter, I believe he is circumcised into the bargain.

CHORUS
O golden news! How say you! pray tell me, for you are proving he hath brought home a whole heap of Money.

CARIO
I think I prove that he hath brought home a heap of the infirmities of old-age.

CHORUS
And do you expect to escape in a whole skin, after imposing on us thus, whilst I have this cudgel in my hand?

CARIO
You think then that I am a person naturally given to such tricks; and nothing but what is stark naught, I warrant you, can come from my mouth.

CHORUS
Observe the gravity of this hang-dog. Sirrah, your shins cry out aloud for the stocks and fetters.

CARIO
Your lot is to distribute justice in the other world; yet you will not set out, tho' Charon hath delivered you your staff.

CHORUS
Burst thy guts for an impudent rascal as thou art, and a cheat in grain, that hast thus imposed on us—and hast had the assurance not yet to tell us on what account thy master sent thee to call us from our work, and made us hasten hither when we had so little leisure, and pass by many good herbs, without gathering any.

CARIO
Well, I will conceal the matter no longer; Plutus then, my good people, is the person my master hath brought home; Plutus, who will make us rich.

CHORUS
Indeed! and is it possible that we shall all become rich?

CARIO
Ay, by the Gods, shall ye, all be Midas's, if you can but each procure a pair of Ass's ears.

CHORUS

How I am delighted! How I am transported, and ready to dance for joy—if all this is really true.

CARIO

And I myself will dance like the Cyclops, Tantararara—and capering thus with my feet, I will lead up myself. Come on, my boys, at every turn bawl and bleat forth the songs of sheep and stinking goats—Come, follow me, and dance as wantonly as ye can, with all the qualifications of a goat.

CHORUS

We'll follow thee bleating, Mr. Tantararara Cyclops; and when we have caught thee, thou hungry cur, with thy satchel full of wild pot-herbs, staggering before thy flock; or, perhaps, when thou art snoring under some hedge, then, sirrah, we will take a swinging staff, and, burning it at one end, blind thee.

CARIO

I will in all things imitate the Circe, who mixed up those drugs, which formerly persuaded the retinue of Philonides at Corinth, as if they were really swine, to eat well-kneaded dung, which she herself kneaded for them; and do you, my little pigs, grunting with delight, follow me, your dam.

CHORUS

Well then, and we, in our merry mood, will take thee, Madam The Circe, mixing up those drugs, enchanting and defiling that retinue, and hang thee up by thy virility; and anoint thy nostrils with thy kneaded dung, till they have the savor of a he-goat; and thou, like gaping Aristyllus, shalt say—Pigs, follow your dam.

CARIO

But, come—now a truce with jesting. Do you return to your former shapes. As for my part, I will steal some bread and meat from my master, and employ the remainder of my leisure in eating; and, when I have filled my belly, will set my hands to the work we are upon.

SCENE II

CHREMYLUS, CHORUS.

CHREMYLUS

To bid you barely welcome, my countrymen, is an old and fusty salutation. I say, I receive you with open arms, since you hasten to me with so much alacrity, and in such good order. Now persevere, and lend me your assistance, that we may be the preservers of this God.

CHORUS

Courage! Imagine you have in me a very Mars before your eyes. It would be a shame indeed, that we, who all of us wrangle so stoutly in our assemblies for a Triobolus, should tamely suffer any one to carry off Plutus from us.

CHREMYLUS

Odso! I see Blepsidemus too coming this way: it is plain, by the haste he is in, he hath heard something of this business.

BLEPSIDEMUS, CHREMYLUS.

BLEPSIDEMUS
What can I make of this? Whence, and by what means, hath Chremylus got all these riches on a sudden? I will not believe it; and yet, by Hercules, it is the public discourse of all the barbers' shops, that he is grown rich in an instant: but to me it is a prodigy, that a man, who hath any good luck, should send for his friends to share it. Surely, he hath done a very unfashionable thing.

CHREMYLUS
By the gods, I will tell him the truth, concealing nothing. O Blepsidemus, our circumstances are finely altered since yesterday; for you are at liberty to share my good fortune, since you are one of my friends!

BLEPSIDEMUS
And are you indeed become rich, as the report goes?

CHREMYLUS
I shall be so very suddenly,—if our God pleases: for there is yet—there is some hazard in the matter.

BLEPSIDEMUS
What hazard?

CHREMYLUS
Why, there is—

BLEPSIDEMUS
Tell me instantly, what is it?

CHREMYLUS
If we are successful, we are made for ever. If we miscarry, we are utterly ruined.

BLEPSIDEMUS
This concern of yours looks ill on your side, and is far from pleasing me; for, to grow extremely rich all on a sudden, and at the same time to be so full of apprehensions, betokens a man who hath committed some heinous crime.

CHREMYLUS
How! some heinous crime!

BLEPSIDEMUS
If you have stolen something from Delphos, whence you are just arrived, either gold or silver belonging to the god, and you now repent of it—

CHREMYLUS
O Apollo, the averter—Not I indeed.

BLEPSIDEMUS
Leave trifling, good old gentleman, I know very well—

CHREMYLUS
Do you suspect such a thing of me?

BLEPSIDEMUS
I know—that there is no man truly honest; we are none of us above the influence of gain.

CHREMYLUS
By Ceres, you seem to me to be out of your senses.

BLEPSIDEMUS [Aside]
How different is this poor man's behaviour from what it was!

CHREMYLUS
By heavens, friend, you are out of your mind.

BLEPSIDEMUS [Aside]
How his eyes wander!—the certain indication of a man who hath committed some knavish prank.

CHREMYLUS
I know what you are croaking to yourself. You think I have stolen something, and want to share in the booty.

BLEPSIDEMUS
I want to share! In what, pray?

CHREMYLUS
But this is no such thing—it is an affair of quite another nature.

BLEPSIDEMUS
O! then you have not stolen, you have taken it away by violence.

CHREMYLUS
The man is possessed.

BLEPSIDEMUS
What, not even cheated any one?

CHREMYLUS
Not I, truly.

BLEPSIDEMUS
O Hercules, which way can a man turn himself in this affair: for I see you will not discover a word of truth.

CHREMYLUS

You accuse me, before you have informed yourself of the nature of my case.

BLEPSIDEMUS

Harkee, friend; I will make this matter up for you very cheap, before the town knows any thing of it. A small matter of money will stop the orators' mouths.

CHREMYLUS

By Jupiter, you appear a very good friend indeed; I suppose you will lay out three minæ, and then charge me twelve.

BLEPSIDEMUS

Methinks, I see a certain person standing at the bar, with his petition in his hand, and his wife and children by him, extremely resembling the picture of the Heraclidæ, as it was drawn by Pamphilus.

CHREMYLUS

I a suppliant! No, thou sot: but henceforward none but the good and worthy, and modest part of mankind, shall be enriched by me.

BLEPSIDEMUS

How say you! What, have you stolen such a prodigious sum?

CHREMYLUS

O villany! Thou wilt ruin—

BLEPSIDEMUS

You will ruin yourself, or I'm mistaken.

CHREMYLUS

Not I: for I have Plutus in my possession, you wretch!

BLEPSIDEMUS

You Plutus! What Plutus?

CHREMYLUS

Plutus, the god of riches.

BLEPSIDEMUS

And where is he?

CHREMYLUS

Within.

BLEPSIDEMUS

Where?

CHREMYLUS

Here, in my house.

BLEPSIDEMUS

In your house!

CHREMYLUS

Even so.

BLEPSIDEMUS

Go hang yourself—Plutus at your house!

CHREMYLUS

Yes, by the gods, is he.

BLEPSIDEMUS

And do you really tell truth?

CHREMYLUS

I do.

BLEPSIDEMUS

Do you, by Vesta?

CHREMYLUS

Yes, and by Neptune too.

BLEPSIDEMUS

What Neptune? do you mean the god of the sea?

CHREMYLUS

Ay, and t'other Neptune too, if there be any other.

BLEPSIDEMUS

What, keep Plutus to yourself, and not send him over to us your friends!

CHREMYLUS

Matters are not yet ripe enough for that.

BLEPSIDEMUS

What, not to communicate him to any one!

CHREMYLUS

No, by Jupiter—we must first—

BLEPSIDEMUS

What must we?

CHREMYLUS

Restore him to his sight.

BLEPSIDEMUS

Restore whom! tell me.

CHREMYLUS

Plutus; and by some means or other, make him see as well as ever.

BLEPSIDEMUS

Is Plutus then really blind?

CHREMYLUS

Ay, by Jove is he.

BLEPSIDEMUS

O! then it is no wonder he never came near my house.

CHREMYLUS

But, by the blessing of the gods, he will come now.

BLEPSIDEMUS

Would it not be proper then to call in the assistance of some physician?

CHREMYLUS

Pray, what physician can there be in this city: for, as there are here no fees for physicians, there is, consequently, no such art.

BLEPSIDEMUS

Let us see, however.

CHREMYLUS

But I tell you there is none.

BLEPSIDEMUS

Nay, I believe so too.

CHREMYLUS

By Jupiter, the best way is to lay him in the temple of Æsculapius, as I myself before intended.

BLEPSIDEMUS

You say true. Be not dilatory: but do something or other immediately.

CHREMYLUS

I am going.

BLEPSIDEMUS

Well, make haste.

CHREMYLUS

I think of nothing else.

SCENE IV

POVERTY, CHREMYLUS, BLEPSIDEMUS.

POVERTY
O ye wretches, possessed with the devil, who dare attempt this bold, wicked, and lawless action—whither, whither do you fly? will you not stop?

CHREMYLUS
O Hercules!

POVERTY
Be assured I will absolutely destroy you, ye wicked wretches, who have dared conceive such an insufferable and audacious attempt; an attempt, which no one, at any time, either god or man, hath ventured on: wherefore you may both conclude yourselves already destroyed.

CHREMYLUS
Who, pray, are you with your terrible pale countenance?

BLEPSIDEMUS
Perhaps, she is a tragical fury belonging to the play-house: for she hath a wild and tragical aspect.

CHREMYLUS
Ay, but she hath no torch in her hand.

BLEPSIDEMUS
If she be no fury, she shall howl for this behaviour.

POVERTY
Whom, pray, do you imagine me to be?

CHREMYLUS
Why, some paltry hostess, or oyster-wench; for else you would not have scolded at us in this manner, without receiving any affront.

POVERTY
Indeed! Why, have you not done me the greatest injury in the world, who have endeavoured to expel me out of this whole country.

CHREMYLUS
Not out of the whole country; there is still the Barathrum left open to you.—But seriously, you had best tell us this very instant who you are?

POVERTY

I am one, who will this day punish you both, for having endeavoured to exterminate me hence.

BLEPSIDEMUS
Oho! is not this she, who keeps the Hedge-Tavern in our neighbourhood, who is constantly ruining me with her bad half-pints.

POVERTY
I am Poverty then, who have dwelt with you both these many years.

BLEPSIDEMUS
O King Apollo, and ye gods, whither may one fly?

CHREMYLUS
What are you doing? What a cowardly animal art thou?—Why don't you stand your ground!

BLEPSIDEMUS
Not by any means.

CHREMYLUS
How! not stay! shall we two men fly from one woman?

BLEPSIDEMUS
But she is Poverty, thou miserable man, than which a more pernicious creature was never produced.

CHREMYLUS
Stand firmly: I beseech thee, stand.

BLEPSIDEMUS
By Jove, but I wont.

CHREMYLUS
Why, I tell you, we shall be guilty of the absurdest of all actions in the world, if we should run away, and leave the god destitute, for fear of this woman here, without daring to contend with her.

BLEPSIDEMUS
In what arms, or what strength shall we confide: for, is there a breast-plate, or even a shield, which this old hag doth not carry to pawn?

CHREMYLUS
Courage! This god alone (I am confident) will triumph over all the tricks of this woman.

POVERTY
Do you presume to mutter, you refuse of mankind, when you have been caught in this detestable undertaking, caught in the very fact.

BLEPSIDEMUS
Why dost thou, while the rod hangs over thee, attack us with thy reproaches, when thou hast not suffered the least injury?

POVERTY

How! in the name of the Gods, do you think you have done me no injury, in endeavouring to restore the eyes of Plutus?

CHREMYLUS

What injury do we do you in this, whilst we are doing so much good to all mankind?

POVERTY

What great good are you contriving?

CHREMYLUS

What good! First, having expelled you out of Greece—

POVERTY

Expelled me! and, pray, what greater mischief can you imagine yourselves able to bring on mankind?

CHREMYLUS

What?—why, by delaying to expel you.

POVERTY

But I am willing, first, to give you a satisfactory account of this matter: and if I demonstrate, that I am the only cause of all the good which happens to you; and it is through me alone you live—Nay, if I dont, then to do to me whatever is agreeable to your pleasure.

CHREMYLUS

And have you the boldness, you hag, to say this?

POVERTY

Nay, be you undeceived: for I shall easily demonstrate you to be utterly mistaken, when you say that you will make honest men rich.

BLEPSIDEMUS

O for some instruments of torture for thee!

POVERTY

You ought not to make this outcry and uproar before you know any thing of the matter.

BLEPSIDEMUS

Who can forbear roaring out, when he hears all this?

POVERTY

Every man of sense can forbear it.

CHREMYLUS

But, if you are cast, what penalty will you be bound to undergo?

POVERTY

Whatever you please.

BLEPSIDEMUS
Now you talk to the purpose.

POVERTY
For if you are cast, you must submit to the same terms.

BLEPSIDEMUS
I suppose twenty hangings will be sufficient.

CHREMYLUS
Ay, for her: but one-a-piece will suffice for us.

POVERTY
This you shall surely suffer, or find some very substantial reply to my allegations.

SCENE V

CHORUS, CHREMYLUS, BLEPSIDEMUS, and **POVERTY.**

CHORUS
It now behoves you to say something very specious on your side; if you will get the better of this antagonist, it will require your utmost abilities.

CHREMYLUS
First then, I am persuaded this is universally acknowledged, that good men are justly entitled to prosperity; and as certainly, that the base and wicked should suffer a contrary fate. We, therefore, having considered this, have, with great difficulty, found out the means to effect an expedient in itself excellent, generous, and most effectual to this purpose: for, if Plutus should be now restored to his sight, instead of strolling blindly about the world, he will then go to the habitations of the good, and never again forsake them: at the same time he will fly the dwellings of the wicked. And thus he will, in the end, make all men good, rich and religious. And now, who can invent an expedient more useful to mankind than this?

BLEPSIDEMUS
No one, surely. I will attest all you say, dont ask her confirmation.

CHREMYLUS
For, as human affairs are now circumstanced, who would not rather call the whole phrenzy, and raving madness! For, how many villains florish in riches, notwithstanding the injustice with which they have accumulated them; and how many of the best of men are in the utmost distress, nay, even starve, and are obliged to spend most of their time in thy company.
[To **POVERTY**]
There is a way, therefore, I say, to stop this mischief; and, if we put Plutus with his eyes open into it, he will effect the greatest advantages for mankind.

POVERTY

You two old dotards, joint companions in folly and madness; you, who of all men are the most easily persuaded to quit the road of sound reason. Should this which you long for, be accomplished, I say, it would not be conducive to your happiness: for, should Plutus recover his sight, and distribute his favors equally, no man would trouble himself with the theory of any art, nor with the exercise of any craft; and if these two should once disappear, who afterwards will become a brasier, a shipwright, a taylor, a wheelwright, a shoemaker, a brick-maker, a dyer, or a skinner? Or who will plough up the bowels of the earth, in order to reap the fruits of Ceres, if it was once possible for you to live with the neglect of all these things.

CHREMYLUS

Ridiculous trifler! our slaves will with their labor perform for us all you have enumerated.

POVERTY

But whence will you have any slaves?

CHREMYLUS

We will purchase them with money, to be sure.

POVERTY

But who will be the seller, when he himself is in no want of money?

CHREMYLUS

O! some Thessalian merchant, or other, amongst those numerous slave-mongers, will be induced by the lust of gain.

POVERTY

But, according to your scheme, there will, in the first place, be no such slave-monger: for what rich man would run the hazard of life in such traffic? You yourself, therefore, will be obliged to plough and to dig, and to undergo all other laborious tasks; so that you will pass your time much worse than at present.

CHREMYLUS

May this evil fall on your own head.

POVERTY

No more shall you sleep on downy beds, or repose on carpets: for none such will be; since no man with his pockets full of money will be a weaver. Nor shall you be perfumed with liquid sweets, not even on your wedding-day; nor adorn yourselves with sumptuous embroidery. What then will avail your riches, when you will be able to purchase none of these things with them: for, as for the necessaries of life, these will be copiously supplied you hy me: for I it is, who standing by the handicraft, compel him, like a mistress, through poverty, and the want of necessaries, to labor for his sustenance.

CHREMYLUS

With what good canst thou supply mankind, except blisters on the legs from the public bagnio-fires, and the cries of half-starved children and old women! together with an army of lice, gnats, and fleas, (too numerous to be mustered) which humming round our heads, torment us, awakening us, and saying, rise, or starve. Moreover, instead of clothes we shall have rags; instead of a bed of down we shall have one of rushes full of bugs, which will awaken us out of the soundest sleep; instead of a carpet we shall have a rotten mat; and instead of a pillow, we shall prop our heads with a stone. As to our food, we shall exchange bread for mallow-branches, and furmety for the leaves of radishes. Our seats will not be chairs, but the head of a broken jar; and lastly, we shall be even compelled to use one side of a broken crutch, instead of a kneading-trough.—Well, madam, do not I demonstrate that you are the author of many blessings to mankind?

POVERTY
You have not been describing my life: but canting forth the life of beggars.

CHREMYLUS
Well: and we commonly say, that poverty is the sister of beggary.

POVERTY
Very well you may, who make no distinction between the tyrant Dionysius and the patriot Thrasybulus. But I never suffered any of these calamities; nor, by Jupiter, am I in any danger of them. The life of a beggar, which you mention, is indeed exposed to every want: but the state of poverty is only confined to frugality and business; and neither wants, nor abounds.

CHREMYLUS
O Ceres! what a blessed life you have described. If after all his parsimony and labor, he shall not leave enough to bury him.

POVERTY
You aim at banter and raillery, and are unwilling to be serious; not knowing that I make better men, both in body and mind, than Plutus; for about him are the gouty, and the tun-bellied, and the dropsy-legged, and men choked with their own fat; but in my train are only the slender, the active, and the most terrible to their enemies.

CHREMYLUS
Very probably! for by starving them you make them slender enough.

POVERTY
Well then, I proceed now to the purity of men's manners, and I shall convince you, that good manners dwell entirely with me; for all abuse belongs to riches.

CHREMYLUS
O certainly! for to steal, and to break open houses, is, no doubt, a very mannerly thing.

BLEPSIDEMUS
Yes, by Jove: it must be certainly very reputable, if the thief be obliged to conceal himself.

BLEPSIDEMUS
Look round among the orators; whilst they are poor, how careful of conserving the rights of the people; but, when they are once enriched with the public money, they immediately part with their honesty; they form designs against their city, and declare war with the people.

CHREMYLUS

Why, there is no great falsehood in this, as malicious a witch as thou art; but you shall not suffer the less; so I would not advise you to swagger: for I will not forgive your endeavor to deceive us into an opinion that poverty is superior to the god of riches.

POVERTY
Nor can you refute a word of what I have said. You trifle only: your wit, like an unfledged bird, can but flutter; it is unable to rise.

CHREMYLUS
But how comes it that all men shun you as they do?

POVERTY
Because I make them better. This may be chiefly perceived in children, who shun their fathers, for advising them to pursue what is most excellent: so difficult is it to distinguish what is right.

CHREMYLUS
You will not, I hope, say, that Jupiter doth not truly distinguish what is right, for he hath riches: but he keeps them to himself, and sends you only to us.

POVERTY
O you dotards, whose minds are blinded with obsolete opinions—Jupiter is most certainly poor—and I will convince you of it plainly: for, if he was rich, would he, when he celebrates the Olympic games, (for which purpose he convenes all Greece every five years) crown with wild olive those whom he proclaims the victorious wrestlers. It would rather become him, if he was rich, to give them a golden crown.

CHREMYLUS
By this instance you see he manifestly shows his respect for riches: for, with the utmost frugality, and hatred to expense, he binds the victors with trifles, and keeps all the riches to himself.

POVERTY
You endeavor to fasten a much greater scandal than poverty on him, by saying he is rich; and at the same time so void of liberality, and so tenacious.

CHREMYLUS
May Jupiter confound thee; but may he first crown thee with wild olive.

POVERTY
For your presuming to contradict me, when I say that poverty is the authoress of all your blessings, may you—

CHREMYLUS
You need only consult Hecate, to know whether wealth or poverty be preferable: she will tell you, that the rich send her in every month a supper; but that the poor snatch it away before it is laid on the table—But go hang yourself, without muttering another word: for, though you should persuade us of the truth, you shall not persuade us to believe you.

POVERTY
O city of Argos, hear what he says.

CHREMYLUS

Call rather for your mess-mate Pauson.

POVERTY

What shall I do? unhappy that I am!

CHREMYLUS

Go hang yourself immediately.

POVERTY

Whither shall I go?

CHREMYLUS

To the pillory. Nay, loiter not—but away with you.

POVERTY

Verily, verily, you will send for me hither again.

CHREMYLUS

When we send for thee thou shalt return: but, at present, go, and be d—d: for riches seem to me much the more eligible; and you may blubber, and tear your hair off with madness, if you please.

BLEPSIDEMUS

For my part, the moment I have got the riches which I have set my heart upon, I will feast it with my wife and children; and then, having washed and perfumed myself, as I return from the bagnio, I will f—t in the faces of all the handicraft-men, and this hag Poverty, wherever I meet her.

SCENE VI

CHREMYLUS, BLEPSIDEMUS.

CHREMYLUS

Well, this goal-bird is gone at last; and now we two will, with the utmost expedition, convey the god into the temple of Æsculapius, and there lay him on a bed.

BLEPSIDEMUS

Let us then lose no time, lest we should meet with a second interruption in our business.

CHREMYLUS

Here, Cario, bring out the blankets, and conduct Plutus himself with all proper ceremonies, and bring too all the other things which are prepared within.

ACT III

CARIO, CHORUS.

CARIO
O yes! All ye happy old men, who in the festivals of Theseus, have been contented with very scanty meals of bread; and all others, who have any honesty in you.

CHORUS
What is the matter, thou best of all thy gang; for thou seemest to be the messenger of some good news.

CARIO
My master hath had some excellent good fortune; or rather indeed, Plutus himself hath had it: for, from blindness, he hath recovered his eyes; ay, not only the sight, but the beauty of them, by the favorable assistance of Æsculapius.

CHORUS
You give me joy, you set me a huzzaing.

CARIO
Yes; joy is come to you now, whether you will or no.

CHORUS
I will halloo forth the praises of Æsculapius, the father of so fine and numerous a progeny, and great light to mankind.

SCENE II

CARIO and the **WIFE** of Chremylus.

WIFE
What can be the meaning of all this hallooing? will it bring us any good tidings; for I have waited within for this Cario a long time, in expectation of them?

CARIO
Quickly, quickly, mistress, give us some wine; that you may drink yourself—(which is, I know, what you dearly love to do) aside : for I bring all manner of blessings to you in a lump.

WIFE
And where are they?

CARIO
You shall soon know them in what I am going to tell you.

WIFE

Dispatch them immediately.

CARIO
Hasten then: for I will deduce the whole affair from foot to head.

WIFE
Deduce nothing on my head, I beseech you.

CARIO
What? not the good things which have just now happened.

WIFE
None of your affairs, I desire.

CARIO
As soon as we arrived at the temple, conducting a man, then in the most miserable condition; but now happy and blessed, if any one is so: first, we led him to the sea, and then washed him.

WIFE
By Jove, he must be truly happy; a poor old fellow, ducked in the cold water.

CARIO
But when we came within the holy precincts, and the loaves, and previous sacrifices were placed on the altar, together with a cake well hardened with fire, we laid Plutus down, and, according to the custom, every one of us fell to making his own bed.

WIFE
What, were there any more of you who wanted the god's assistance?

CARIO
There was only one, Neoclides by name; who is indeed blind, but in thieving hath always out-shot those who can see. There were likewise many others afflicted with various diseases. At length the sacristan having put out the lights, ordered us to fall asleep; and charged us, if we heard any noise not to cry out. We then laid down all of us in a very orderly manner: but I could not sleep. A pot of pease-porridge, which lay at a little distance from an old woman's head, had a violent effect on my nostrils: indeed, I had a supernatural motion to creep towards it; when looking up, I saw the priest greedily snatching away the cakes and figs from the sacred table: after which he took his rounds about the altars, to see if there was any loaf left, and consecrated all he found into a wallet, which he carried for that purpose; upon which, I, thinking this was a great act of devotion, stood up in my turn to the porridge-pot.

WIFE
O thou wretch, hadst thou no apprehension of the god?

CARIO
Yes, by all the gods, had I, an apprehension, that, having his garlands on, he would get to the pot before me: for that the priest had told me before-hand. As for the old woman, when she heard the noise, she put out her hand to secure her porridge; I, hissing like one of Æsculapius's serpents, seized it in my teeth; upon which she immediately drew it back into her bed, and wrapping herself up close, very

quietly laid down till she outstunk a cat, f—ting with fear; but I then fell to supping up the pease-porridge. When my belly was full, I betook myself to my repose.

WIFE
But, did not the god appear to you?

CARIO
No, not yet. After this I did a very merry thing: for, as the god was approaching, I let a loud f—t; for my belly was cursedly puffed up with the porridge.

WIFE
For which he certainly held thee in the utmost abhorrence.

CARIO
No, but his daughter Jaso, as she attended her father, reddened a little; and her sister Panacea turned away her head, holding her nose; for I assure you I f—t no frankincense.

WIFE
But Æsculapius himself—what did he?

CARIO
O by Jove, he never troubled his head about it.

WIFE
Surely, according to your account, this god hath very little regard to good manners.

CARIO
My account!—I say the gold finders and he live upon the same commodity.

WIFE
O wretch!

CARIO
After this, I presently covered myself up, out of fear; and he very decently went his rounds, and inspected all the cases: immediately afterwards his apprentice brought him his stone mortar, and his pestle, and his box.

WIFE
What! a stone-box?

CARIO
No, by Hercules! not the box, but the mortar was of stone.

WIFE
Sure, some terrible judgment will fall on thy head: for, how could you see all these things, when you say you had covered your head in the bed-clothes?

CARIO

I saw all through the hole of my cloak; and, by Jupiter, there are windows enow in it. The first operation was performed on Neoclides, for whom the god ordered his apprentice to pound an ointment in a mortar, throwing in three heads of garlick of Tenos; which being done, he himself mixed it with benjamin and mastic, and then adding some vinegar of Sphettus, he spread the plaister, and put it on, having first turned his eye-lids outwards, that he might put him to the greater torment. Poor Neoclides first squalled, then roared, then took to his heels, and ran away full speed: at which the god laughing heartily, said to him, sit quietly down with your plaister; I will take care you shall keep your oath, and abstain from the courts of justice.

WIFE

What a wise deity this is, and what a lover of the people!

CARIO

He then sat down by Plutus. And first he stroked his head; next, taking a clean napkin, he wiped round his eye-lids. Panacea now covered his head and face with a scarlet cloth, after which the god whistled; immediately two serpents of a supernatural size rushed forth from the sacred part of the temple.

WIFE

O good God!

CARIO

And these creeping softly under the scarlet cloth, fell a licking the eye-lids; at least so it seemed to me: and in less time than you could drink off ten half-pints of wine, Plutus, (I assure you, Madam, it is true,) was started up with his eyes open. I clapped my hands for joy, and wakened my master; presently the god disappeared, and the serpents returned into the inmost recesses of the temple. Now several of those who lay near him fell to embracing him with inexpressible affection, and kept awake till it was broad day-light. I uttered vehement praises of the god, for having so suddenly restored Plutus his eyes, and made Neoclides blinder than before.

WIFE

O Æsculapius, what a powerful deity art thou! but, tell me, what is become of Plutus?

CARIO

He is coming: but there is a prodigious crowd gathered about him. Those who had led honest lives, and been poor, embraced him, and all received him with much pleasure; but those who had dishonestly acquired great substance, knitted their brows, and looked very sour. Whereas the former, crowned with garlands, followed behind, laughing, and shouting. The shoes of the elders resounded as they went; for they advanced, beating time, as it were, with their feet: come on, my boys, with one accord, every man of you, dance and caper, and figure in; for no man will hereafter tell us, when we enter his house, that there is no pudding in the pot.

WIFE

O Hecate, I will crown thee—with a string of buns for this good news.

CARIO

Make no longer delay; for the men are near our door.

WIFE

Well, I go in, and will fetch the customary entertainment, to welcome his new-purchased eyes.

CARIO
And I will go and meet the procession.

PLUTUS, **CHREMYLUS**, and his **WIFE**.

PLUTUS
First, I pay my adoration to the sun; then I salute the illustrious soil of the venerable Pallas, and all the country of Cecrops, which hath hospitably received me. I blush at my misfortunes, when I recollect with what men I have ignorantly passed my time, and have shunned those, who were only worthy of my conversation. Unhappy as I was, who knew nothing of the matter all this while. How wrong have I been in both; but, for the future, turning over a new leaf, I will show all mankind, that it was against my will I gave up myself to the wicked.

CHREMYLUS
Go, and be hanged, all of you—what troublesome things are friends, who immediately appear, when any good fortune attends you! They tread on my heels, and squeeze me to death, every one expressing his affection for me: for, who hath not spoken to me! with what a crowd of elders have I been surrounded in the Forum!

WIFE
Your humble servant, dear Sir,
[To **PLUTUS**]
—and yours, Sir,—
(To her **HUSBAND**]
—Give me leave, Sir, according to our custom, to welcome you with this entertainment.

PLUTUS
By no means: for, at my entrance into your house, on the recovery of my sight, it becomes me better to make you a present than to receive one.

WIFE
Will you be so unkind not to accept it?

PLUTUS
Not till I am at your fire-side: for there it is the custom to receive it. After I have got clear of this troublesome crowd: for it becomes not our poet to throw figs and sweetmeats among the spectators, in order to bribe their applause.

WIFE
You say very true: for, yonder I see stand up Xenicus ready to scramble for the figs.

CARIO

How sweet is it, Sirs, to get riches, without sending out any ventures for them! How is a whole heap of good things rushed in upon us, without doing the least evil! Riches, so acquired, are indeed a blessing.—Our bin is full of fine flour; our vessels, of black sweet-flavored wine; our trunks, of gold and silver! Well, it is wonderful! Our well is full of oil, our oil-cruises are filled with precious ointment! Our garret with figs! Every vinegar-jar, and tray, and pot, are all become of shining brass! Our fish platters, which were of wood, and something rotten, are now all silver! Our dresser is of a sudden become ivory! we servants now play at even and odd with golden staters, and are so elegant, that we wipe our posteriors with garlic, instead of stones. And now my master, with a garland on his head, is sacrificing within, a hog, a goat, and a ram; the smoke hath sent me out: for I was able to bear it no longer, it so offended my eyes.

DICÆUS and **CARIO**.

DICÆUS [Speaking to a YOUTH]
Follow me, my child, and let us go together to the god.

CARIO
Hey dey! who comes here?

DICÆUS
One, who was miserable; but is now fortunate.

CARIO
O then, certainly you are of the number of good men, as it should seem.

DICÆUS
Most certainly.

CARIO
And what do you want?

DICÆUS
I am going to the god; who is the author of great blessings to me. You must know, that I, having inherited a very sufficient fortune from my father, supplied my necessitous friends with it: for I thought it the surest way to secure to myself a comfortable life.

CARIO
No doubt you soon saw the bottom of your purse.

DICÆUS
You are in the right.

CARIO
You were then certainly miserable.

DICÆUS
Even so. But I thought, when I assisted them in their necessity, that I should find them friends indeed, if I should ever want any; whereas, when that day came, they turned their backs, and pretended not to see me.

CARIO
Ay, and I make no doubt laughed heartily at you into the bargain.

DICÆUS
Very true. I was almost destroyed by the drought—of my dishes.

CARIO
But it is not so now with you?

DICÆUS
No: for which reason I am come to the god to offer my adoration, as I ought.

CARIO
But this old cloak here—what, in the name of Jupiter, is the meaning of this old cloak, which the boy carries after you?—Pray tell me.

DICÆUS
I intend to dedicate it to the god.

CARIO
I hope you were not initiated into the great mysteries in this—

DICÆUS
No, but I have shivered in it these thirteen years.

CARIO
And those old shoes there?

DICÆUS
And these have spent the winter with me.

CARIO
And do you dedicate these too?

DICÆUS
Yes, by Jove.

CARIO

You have brought most grateful offerings to the deity, no doubt.

SYCOPHANTES, CARIO, and **DICÆUS**.

SYCOPHANTES

O unhappy and undone man that I am! O thrice unhappy, and four times, and five times, and twelve times, and ten thousand times—O! O! of what a variety of ills is my fortune composed!

CARIO

Apollo, and all propitious Deities defend us! What terrible misfortune hath happened to this man!

SYCOPHANTES

Have not the greatest misfortunes fallen on me this day; who am, by the means of this god, stripped of every thing I had in the world? But, if there be any justice upon earth, I'll have him restored to his former blindness again.

DICÆUS

I begin to smell the matter. This man is certainly in a very bad way; but he hath a very bad stamp on his countenance.

CARIO

If he is a rascal, I think, when he is in the road to destruction, he may be said to be in a very fair way.

SYCOPHANTES

Where is he! where is the traitor! who promised to-day, that, when he had recovered his eyes, he would alone make us all rich; and now he hath them, he puts some of us into a worse condition than we were in before!

CARIO

Whom, pray, hath he served so?

SYCOPHANTES

Whom! why me myself.

CARIO

You! Ay, but you are a rogue, and a house-breaker.

SYCOPHANTES

No, Sirrah! but there is not a grain of honesty in such fellows as you—nor is it possible but you must have robbed me of my money.

CARIO

Bless me! what a magisterial air the Sycophant advances to us with.

DICÆUS DICAEUS
The man is plainly perishing with hunger.

SYCOPHANTES [To **CARIO**]
Come, you Sir, this instant, into court: you shall be put on the wheel, and racked till you confess all your rogueries.

CARIO
You be racked yourself!

DICÆUS
By Jupiter the preserver; this god is worthy of the highest honor from all Greece; for exacting such just vengeance of Sycophants.

SYCOPHANTES
What a wretch am I!—Ha! do you too laugh at me, after having a share in the plunder! for whence could you otherwise come by this fine coat; you, whom yesterday I saw wrapped up in a miserable old cloak!

DICÆUS
I regard you not. See on my finger this amulet-ring, which I bought of Eudamus for a drachma.

CARIO
There are no charms in your ring against the bite of a Sycophant.

SYCOPHANTES
I think this very injurious treatment: you revile me, but will not tell me what is your business: for you are here on no good design, I am certain.

CARIO
With no design for your good, you may be well assured of that.

SYCOPHANTES
By Jupiter, but you will sup to-night at my expense.

DICÆUS
May this be true; and may you and your witness burst your bellies—but not with meat.

SYCOPHANTES [Sniffling]
Do you deny it, you villains, when I smell such a flavor of fish and roast-meat from within? phu, phu, phu.

CARIO
What do you smell, sirrah?

DICÆUS
I suppose he smells the cold: for his clothes are in a very tattered condition.

SYCOPHANTES

This is insufferable. O Jupiter, and all you gods! are these fellows to insult me! how my indignation rises, that an honest man, and a patriot, should be reduced to such a condition.

DICÆUS

You an honest man, and a patriot!

SYCOPHANTES

Yes, no other comes near me.

DICÆUS

Answer me a few questions.

SYCOPHANTES

What are they?

DICÆUS

Are you a farmer?

SYCOPHANTES

Do you think me such a madman?

DICÆUS

You are a merchant then, I suppose.

SYCOPHANTES

I pretend to be so, when I see occasion.

DICÆUS

What then?—Have you learned any handicraft?

SYCOPHANTES

No, by Jove.

DICÆUS

How do you live then, if you do nothing for your livelihood?

SYCOPHANTES

I am a superintendant of the public weal, and of the good of every private person.

DICÆUS

You! and how came you, pray, to take this office upon you?

SYCOPHANTES

Such is my will and pleasure.

DICÆUS

Thou villain! dost thou pretend to be an honest man, who art odious to every one, by doing what doth not belong to you?

SYCOPHANTES
Doth it not belong to me, thou gull, to serve my country with all my might?

DICÆUS
Is an officious meddling with every man's business serving your country?

SYCOPHANTES
Yes, to assist the dead letter of the law; and not to suffer those who offend it to escape with impunity.

DICÆUS
The public takes care to provide proper judges.

SYCOPHANTES
But who will inform?

DICÆUS
Whoever pleases.

SYCOPHANTES
I am then that he, and thus the affairs of the city devolve on me.

DICÆUS
The city hath indeed a sorry protector. Would it not be better for thee to live quietly and peaceably, and intermeddle in nobody's affairs?

SYCOPHANTES
You describe the life of a silly sheep: for such is the life of a man without business.

DICÆUS
You are resolved then not to reform.

SYCOPHANTES
No, not if you would give me Plutus himself, and all the benjamin in Cyrene.

DICÆUS
Off with your cloak immediately.

CARIO
The gentleman speaks to you, Sir.

DICÆUS
And your shoes too.

CARIO
It is all to you, Sir.

SYCOPHANTES
Touch me either of you, whoever pleases.

CARIO
I am then that he.

[Here **CARIO** lays hold on the **INFORMER**, and strips him, at which his witness runs away.

SYCOPHANTES
What a wretch am I, to be thus stripped in open day-light!

DICAEUS
This is your punishment for seeking a scandalous livelihood, by meddling with what doth not belong to you.

SYCOPHANTES
Take care what you do; for I have a witness present.

CARIO
No, sirrah, your witness hath taken to his heels.

SYCOPHANTES
Ha! Wo is me! am I then left alone?

CARIO
What, now you roar?

SYCOPHANTES
Wo is me! I say again.

CARIO
Lend me your old cloak then, that I may cover the gentleman's nakedness.

DICÆUS
By no means. It is already sacred to Plutus.

CARIO
How can it be offered more properly than on the shoulders of this rogue and robber? Plutus should be adorned with rich clothes.

DICÆUS
But tell me to what use shall we put these old shoes?

CARIO
I will nail them up to his forehead, as you nail offerings against the wild olive-tree.

SYCOPHANTES

I will depart; for I see you are too many for me: but, as soon as I find any of my evidences, though never so bad a one, I will bring this god, stout as he is, to condign punishment this very day: for this single fellow manifestly subverts the government, and all without obtaining any authority from the senate or people.

DICÆUS

Well, Sir, since you march in my furniture, make as much haste as you can to the bagnio-fire, that you may get the first place, and warm yourself. It is a post I myself have often stood centry at.

CARIO

The master of the bagnio will lug him out by the heels: he will know him the moment he sees him; for the fellow hath rogue written in his face—But come, let us two go in, that you may pay your adoration to the Deity.

SCENE IV

OLD WOMAN, CHORUS, CHREMYLUS.

OLD WOMAN

Tell me, honest friends, are we indeed arrived at the house of this new Deity, or have we missed our way?

CHORUS

Know, my pretty miss, you ask in very good time; for you are arrived at the very door.

OLD WOMAN

Well then, shall I call some-body out?

CHREMYLUS

There is no need of calling any one; for I am just come out myself: but it will be necessary for you to tell me your business.

OLD WOMAN

O Sir! I have suffered very great and sad mischiefs indeed; for ever since this god here hath recovered his eye-sight, I have had a most uncomfortable life.

CHREMYLUS

What is this? you are an informeress, I suppose.

OLD WOMAN

Not I, by all that is sacred!

CHREMYLUS

What, I suppose, you never had the good fortune to be toast-mistress at your club?

OLD WOMAN

You banter me: but, alas! I am troubled with a terrible itch.

CHREMYLUS
What itch? discover quickly, what itch?

OLD WOMAN
Listen then. I had a dear young fellow, poor indeed he was, but a handsome well-shaped lad, and good-natured; for he supplied all my wants, in the modestest, and prettiest manner: and I, on the other hand, supplied him with all these necessaries—

CHREMYLUS
What were the necessaries, pray, which he chiefly used to want of you?

OLD WOMAN
Not many: for he was a bashful youth, and had a most awful respect for me—He would ask me twenty drachmas to buy him a coat, and eight to buy him a pair of shoes. And he would ask me to buy a cheap gown for his sisters, and a poor wrapper for his mother. Sometimes he would beg four medimni of wheat of me.

CHREMYLUS
By Apollo, what you tell me is no great matter; it is indeed plain he had a most awful respect for you.

OLD WOMAN
And these things, he constantly told me, he did not ask as the reward of his performances, but out of pure friendship, that he might wear my coat for my sake, and remember me by it.

CHREMYLUS
This young fellow, by your account, must have been most desperately in love with you.

OLD WOMAN
Ah! the impudent varlet is not now of the same mind, but is exceedingly altered; for, upon my sending him this cheesecake, and a whole saucer full of sweetmeats, with an assignation, that I would come to him in the evening—

CHREMYLUS
What did he do?—tell me.

OLD WOMAN
He returned me the cheesecake, intending, that I should come no more thither to him; nay, and besides all this, he ordered the messenger to tell me, that the Milesians were formerly stout fellows.

CHREMYLUS
It is plain this young fellow hath not a depraved taste; since now he is grown rich, he delights no longer in lentils: for formerly his poverty obliged him to take up with any dish he could procure.

OLD WOMAN
And yet I swear to you, by the twin gods, he formerly used to walk every day by my door.

CHREMYLUS

What looking for your corpse!

OLD WOMAN

No, only for the pleasure of hearing my voice.

CHREMYLUS

Bidding him take something, I suppose.

OLD WOMAN

And then, if ever he found me in a fit of the vapors, he would caress me by the fond names of my little duck, and my little dove.

CHREMYLUS

And then, perhaps, he would ask you for a pair of shoes.

OLD WOMAN

When I have rode out in my chariot, on the day of celebrating the great mysteries, I have been sure of a hearty thrashing, if any young fellow took it into his head to ogle me: so violently jealous of me was this sweet youth.

CHREMYLUS

It seems then he liked to eat alone.

OLD WOMAN

My hands were, he said, extremely beautiful.

CHREMYLUS

When they held out twenty drachmas to him.

OLD WOMAN

And my skin, he said, had a most delicate smell.

CHREMYLUS

Very probably while you poured forth Thasian wine.

OLD WOMAN

That I had a soft and lovely eye.

CHREMYLUS

This was no awkward fellow, I find—he knows how to feed upon a rampant old woman.

OLD WOMAN

The god, therefore, my good friend, doth not do well; though he pretends that he will redress the wrongs of the injured.

CHREMYLUS

Tell me what you would have him do, and it shall be done immediately.

OLD WOMAN

It is surely reasonable, that he should compel this young man, to whom I have done so much good, to return some good offices to me, otherwise it is not just he should enjoy any advantage whatever.

CHREMYLUS

What! did he not make you a suitable return every night?

OLD WOMAN

Ay, but he promised never to leave me, whilst I was alive.

CHREMYLUS

True! but he now thinks you alive no longer.

OLD WOMAN

Indeed, friend, I am considerably pined away with trouble.

CHREMYLUS

You seem rather to be pined away with rottenness.

OLD WOMAN

You may draw me through a ring.

CHREMYLUS

Ay, if it was as big as a hoop.

OLD WOMAN

As I live, here comes the very youth I have been all this while accusing; he seems to be come a reveling.

CHREMYLUS

He doth so; for he hath a garland and a torch with him.

SCENE V

NEANISCUS, OLD WOMAN, CHREMYLUS.

NEANISCUS

Save you good people.

OLD WOMAN

What says he?

NEANISCUS

My old friend, you are grown grey all on a sudden.

OLD WOMAN

What a wretch am I, to be thus abused!

CHREMYLUS
It seems he hath not seen you a long while.

OLD WOMAN
How long, sirrah!—he was at my house but yesterday.

CHREMYLUS
I find drink hath a contrary effect on him to what it hath on others; it makes him see the clearer.

OLD WOMAN
No; but he is always saucy in his behavior.

NEANISCUS
O Sea-Neptune, and all ye antique gods, what a number of wrinkles she hath in her forehead!

[Holding his torch up to her face.

OLD WOMAN
Ah! Oh! don't thrust your torch in my face.

CHREMYLUS
She is in the right: for, if a single spark should seize her, she will burn like a dry olive-branch.

NEANISCUS
Are you willing we should have a little play together, after this long absence?

OLD WOMAN
Where, wretch?

NEANISCUS
Here, with these walnuts.

OLD WOMAN
What play?

NEANISCUS
How many teeth have you?

CHREMYLUS
I will have my guess. Perhaps, she hath three or four.

NEANISCUS
Pay me: she wears but one, and that is a grinder.

OLD WOMAN
Sure, you are out of your senses, villains, to endeavour before so many men to besprinkle me thus with

your jests.

NEANISCUS
Sprinkle you!—I am sure you would be the better for it, if you was well washed.

CHREMYLUS
No, truly: for she is now varnished over; but should the paint be once washed away, the furrows of her face will appear plain.

OLD WOMAN
As old a man as you are, you seem to me a very simple fellow.

NEANISCUS
Perhaps, he is tempting you. I suppose he doth not think I see him playing with your pretty bubbies.

OLD WOMAN
No, by Venus, you rascal, he touches not mine.

CHREMYLUS
Not I, by Hecate! I am not so simple: but, harkee, young gentleman, you must not have such an aversion to this lass.

NEANISCUS
I! I dote on her!

CHREMYLUS
Why, she accuses you.

NEANISCUS
Of what doth she accuse me?

CHREMYLUS
She says you are insolent, and have told her, that the Milesians were formerly stout fellows.

NEANISCUS
I will not fight with you for her.

CHREMYLUS
Why, pray?

NEANISCUS
In respect to your age; for I should permit this in no other: but, as you are, you may go off safely, and carry the lass along with you.

CHREMYLUS
I well know your meaning—you will not now vouchsafe to converse with her, as you have.

OLD WOMAN

Who is he, who is so free to deliver me up?

NEANISCUS
I do not choose a conversation with one who hath been embraced by thirteen thousand years.

CHREMYLUS
But, since you have drank the wine, you ought to drink the dregs also.

NEANISCUS
Ay, but these are very old and fusty indeed.

CHREMYLUS
Well then, a strainer will cure all that.

NEANISCUS
But go in: for I am desirous to consecrate these crowns to the god.

OLD WOMAN
And I too have something to say to him.

NEANISCUS
But I will not go in.

CHREMYLUS
Courage, man, never fear; she shant ravish you.

NEANISCUS
You speak very kindly: for I have sufficiently pitched up the old vessel already.

OLD WOMAN
Enter; and I will follow you behind.

CHREMYLUS
O king Jupiter, how closely the old woman sticks to the youth, even as a limpet doth to the rock!

ACT V

SCENE I

CARIO, MERCURY.

MERCURY knocks hard at the door, and then retires.

CARIO
Who knocks at the door?—Heyday! What is the meaning of this? Here is nobody.—What, hath the door made all this lamentation, when no-body hurt it!

MERCURY

You, you, Cario; I speak to you, stay.

CARIO

Pray tell me, sir, was it you that knocked so heartily at our door?

MERCURY

Not I, by Jove! but I should have knocked had not you prevented me, by opening it; but run quickly and call your master hither; and then call his wife and children; then his servants, then the bitch, then yourself, and then the sow.

CARIO

Pray, what is the meaning of all this?

MERCURY

Jupiter, sirrah, intends to make a hotchpotch of you altogether, and then souse you into the Barathrum.

CARIO

Such criers as you, truly deserve a tongue cut out: but wherefore, pray, is he contriving this for us?

MERCURY

Because you have committed the most horrible of all facts: for ever since Plutus hath recovered a glimpse of sight, no one hath sacrificed to the gods any frankincense, or laurel, or cake, or any victim; or, in short, any thing at all.

CARIO

No, faith! nor will not either: for I am sure you have taken very little care of us.

MERCURY

Well, as for the other gods, I trouble not myself much: but I myself am ruined and undone.

CARIO

Why, this is modestly spoken.

MERCURY

Formerly I received every morning all kind of good things from the tavern-women, such as wine-cakes, honey, figs, as much as was decent for Mercury to eat: but now I go all day hungry, and have nothing to do but stretch out my legs, and sleep.

CARIO

Very justly: since, notwithstanding all these good things, you often made losers of those who gave them you.

MERCURY

O miserable deity!—O for that cheesecake, which used to be dressed for me on the fourth day of the moon.

CARIO

You desire one who is absent, and call for him in vain.

MERCURY

O! for a gammon of bacon, which I used to feed on.

CARIO

Leap upon the bottle here in the open air.

MERCURY

O those meals of tripe, which I have made?

CARIO

The wind in your own tripes turns your meditations that way.

MERCURY

O those cups of wine and water equally mixed up!

CARIO

You shall not stir till you have drank this cup also.

MERCURY

Will you assist one, who hath a great friendship for you?

CARIO

Ay, if you want any thing within my capacity of helping you to.

MERCURY

If you would but give me one of those well-baked loaves, and a piece of that flesh you are sacrificing within.

CARIO

But they must not be conveyed out.

MERCURY

Why, when you used to filch any vessel from your master, I always assisted you in concealing it.

CARIO

Ay, you rascal; that you might partake in the booty: for a well-baked cake came always to your share.

MERCURY

Ay, but you eat it afterwards yourself.

CARIO

Well: for you had no share in the whipping, when I was taken in my rogueries.

MERCURY

No remembrance of past injuries now Phyle is taken. So pray receive me into your house, in the name of the gods, and let me dwell with you.

CARIO
What, will you leave the gods to dwell with us?

MERCURY
Yes indeed will I: for your affairs are in a much better situation.

CARIO
But in what light do you esteem a man who deserts from his country?

MERCURY
That is every man's country, where he lives best.

CARIO
Well, but what advantage would you bring to us, if you were here?

MERCURY
I will be your turnkey, and stand behind your door.

CARIO
Turnkey!—No, we want none of your turns.

MERCURY
Employ me then in my mercantile capacity.

CARIO
But we are rich, what then should we do with such a huckster as Mercury?

MERCURY
In my crafty vocation then.

CARIO
We have done with craft. Honesty is for our purpose.

MERCURY
You know me to be a conductor.

CARIO
No, the god hath his eyes now, and wants no conductor.

MERCURY
Odso! I will be master of your sports—will not that do?—This is an office, which I am sure will be very convenient for Plutus: for rich men often make matches between musicians and prize-fighters.

CARIO
How useful it is to have various occupations: for by one or the other this fellow hath found out a livelihood: it is not without reason, I find, that our judges put in as many tickets with their names as they

can.

MERCURY
Will nothing that I have said gain me admittance?

CARIO
Yes, yes; come to the well, and wash some guts for me; then you will show yourself to be a good scullion.

PRIEST of Jupiter, **CARIO**.

PRIEST
Who can direct me to the very door where Chremylus lives?

CARIO
What is the matter, honest gentleman?

PRIEST
No good, I assure you, sir. Since this Plutus first recovered his eyes, I have been perishing with hunger: for, indeed, I have not a morsel to eat; and this, though I am the priest of Jupiter the Protector.

CARIO
And what is the reason of this, pray?

PRIEST
No person thinks proper to sacrifice any longer.

CARIO
On what account?

PRIEST
Because they are all rich; whereas formerly, when they were poor, the merchant returning from his voyage offered up his victim: the rogue who escaped out of the hands of justice did the same; and when any one made a handsome sacrifice, he invited the priest to it: but now there is not one who sacrifices, no, not the least matter in the world; nor even comes near the temple, unless those thousands who come there to lay their cates.

CARIO
And have you not your lawful share of these?

PRIEST
As to Jupiter the Protector, I think proper to take my leave of him, and abide here with you.

CARIO

Courage! all will be well, if the god pleases: for the Jupiter the Protector is within already: he came hither of his own accord.

PRIEST
You now tell me delightful news indeed.

CARIO
We shall presently place (bear it with patience) Plutus where your Jupiter was formerly placed, to preserve the treasure which is behind the temple of Minerva.—But give me those lighted torches there, somebody.—Here, priest, do you take them, and carry them before the god.

PRIEST
We are doing no more than we ought.

CARIO
Now call Plutus out.

SCENE III

OLD WOMAN, CARIO, CHORUS.

OLD WOMAN
What shall I do?

CARIO
Take these pots, with which we are to place the god in the temple, carry them on your head with a grave countenance. I see you have already your flowered gown on.

OLD WOMAN
Ay, but of that which I came hither for—

CARIO
All shall be immediately done for you. The young fellow shall be with you in the evening.

OLD WOMAN
Well, if you will be bound that the youth shall visit me, I will carry the pots.

CARIO [Turning to the **SPECTATORS**]
These pots are the very reverse of all others: for in all others the scum used to be at the top of the pot, here it is at the bottom.

CHORUS
There is no reason why we should stay here longer, but follow behind: for it is usual to bring up the rear with a song.

Henry Fielding was born at Sharpham Park, near Glastonbury, in Somerset on April 22nd 1707. His early years were spent on his parents' farm in Dorset. His family were well to do. His father was a colonel, later a general in the army, his maternal grandfather was a judge of the Queen's Bench and his second cousin would later become the fourth Earl of Denbigh.

He was educated at Eton where he became lifelong friends with William Pitt the Elder.

An early romance ended disastrously and with it his removal to London and the beginnings of a glittering literary career. Early advice on this came from another cousin, the noted poet, Lady Mary Wortley Montagu. Fielding published his first play, at age 21, in 1728.

Later that same year he journeyed to the University at Leiden, the oldest University in Holland, to study classics and law. However, within months, with funds low, mainly due to his father cutting off his allowance, he was forced to return to London and to write for the theatre.

It was a twist of fate that was to ensure him both notoriety and a reputation that would exceed his wildest expectations.

He was prolific, sometimes writing six plays a year, but he did like to poke fun at the authorities. His plays were thought to be the final straw for the authorities in their attempts to bring some sense of order to an increasingly provocative Theatre. Some of the plays denigrated, insulted, or criticised either the King, or his Government, in ways that caused them to react with their preferred response; a new law. Although the Golden Rump was cited as the play on which the authorities based their need for better regulation it is thought that the constant stepping over the line by Fielding in his own works was the actual trigger for, and target of, the new law. No copy of the play, The Golden Rump, exists today and it seems never, in fact, to have been performed or perhaps even published. Various accounts attribute Fielding as the author and others say it was secretly commissioned by Walpole himself to bring about the conditions necessary to bring the Act before Parliament.

Whatever the validity in 1737 The Theatrical Licensing Act was passed. At a stroke political satire was almost impossible. Fielding much admired – and reviled – for his savaging of Sir Robert Walpole government was rendered mute. Any playwright who was viewed with suspicion by the Government now found an audience difficult to find and therefore Theatre owners now toed the Government line, works only being available for performance after review by the Lord Chamberlain. A process that was to last in England, although greatly amended in 1843, until 1968.

Fielding was practical in the circumstances and ironically stopped writing to once again take up his career in the practice of law. He became a barrister after studying at Middle Temple – he completed the six year course in only three. By this time he had also married Charlotte Craddock, his first wife, and they would go on to have five children, but only a daughter would survive. Charlotte died in 1744 but was immortalised as the heroine in both Tom Jones and Amelia.

As a businessman Fielding lacked any financial education and he and his family often endured bouts of poverty. He did however find a wealthy benefactor in the shape of Ralph Allen, who was to later feature in the novel Tom Jones as the character foundation for Squire Allworthy.

Fielding never stopped writing political satire or satires of current arts and letters. The Tragedy of Tragedies, for which Hogarth designed the frontispiece, had, for example, some success as a printed play. He also contributed a number of works to journals of the day as well as writing for Tory periodicals, usually under the name of "Captain Hercules Vinegar". His choice of name reveals his style. But then again his other later nom de plumes are also revealing; Sir Alexander Drawcansir and Scriblerus Secundus

In 1731 Fielding wrote "The Roast Beef of Old England", which is used by the Royal Navy and the United States Marine Corps. It was later arranged by Richard Leveridge.

During the late 1730s and early 1740s Fielding continued to air his liberal and anti-Jacobite views in satirical articles and newspapers. He was nothing if not passionate and this adherence to principles would eventually have great reward for him.

Fielding was much put out by the success of Samuel Richardson's Pamela, or Virtue Rewarded. His reaction was to spur him into writing a novel. In 1741 this first novel, Shamela, was a success, an anonymous parody of Richardson's melodramatic novel. It is a satire that follows the model of the famous Tory satirists of the previous generation; Swift and Gay.

On the tail of this success came Joseph Andrews in 1742. Begun as a parody on Pamela's brother, Joseph, it swiftly developed and matured into an accomplished novel in its own right and marked the entrance of Fielding as a major English novelist.

In 1743, he published a novel in the Miscellanies volume III (which was, in fact, the first volume of the Miscellanies). This was The History of the Life of the Late Mr Jonathan Wild the Great. Sometimes this is cited as his first novel, as he did indeed begin writing it before Shamela, but it is now placed later. Once again Fielding returns to satire and one of his favourite subjects – Sir Robert Walpole. In it he draws a parallel between Walpole and Jonathan Wild, the infamous gang leader and highwayman. He implicitly compares the Whig party in Parliament to a gang of thieves, whose leader, Walpole, lives only for his desire and ambition to be a "Great Man" (a common epithet for Walpole) and should culminate only in the antithesis of greatness: being hung from a gallows. By now Walpole had resigned as Prime minster after some 20 years. Fielding could now re-affirm political allegiance back to the Whigs and would now denounce both Tories and Jacobites in his writings.

Although Fielding was never afraid to court controversy he published his next work anonymously in 1746, and perhaps with good reason. The Female Husband, a fictionalized account of a sensational case of a female transvestite who was tried for duping another woman into marriage. This was one of a number of small published pamphlets at sixpence a time. Though a minor item in both length and his canon it shows Fielding's consistent interest and examination of fraud, sham, and masks but, of course, his subject matter was rather sensational.

In 1747, three years after Charlotte's death and ignoring public opinion, he married her former maid, Mary Daniel, who was pregnant. Mary bore him five children altogether; three daughters, who died early and sons William and Allen.

Undoubtedly the masterpiece of Fielding's career was the novel Tom Jones, published in 1749. It is a wonderfully and carefully constructed picaresque novel following the convoluted and hilarious tale of how a foundling came into a fortune.

Fielding was a consistent anti-Jacobite and a keen supporter of the Church of England. This led to him now being richly rewarded with the position of London's Chief Magistrate. The position itself had no salary attached but he refused all manner of bribes during his tenure, which was most unusual. Fielding continued to write and his career both literary and professional continued to climb.

In 1749 he joined with his younger half-brother John, to help found what was the nascent forerunner to a London police force, the Bow Street Runners. (He and his siblings were quite some partnership. His younger sister, Sarah, also became a well known novelist)

His influence here was undoubted. He and John did much to help the cause of judicial reform and to help improve prison conditions. His pamphlets and enquiries included a proposal for the abolition of public hangings. This was not, as you would think because he was opposed to capital punishment as such—indeed, for example, in his 1751 presiding over the trial of the notorious criminal James Field, he found him guilty in a robbery and sentenced him to hang.

In January 1752 Fielding started a fortnightly periodical titled The Covent-Garden Journal, which he would publish under the colourful pseudonym of "Sir Alexander Drawcansir, Knt. Censor of Great Britain" until November of the same year. In this periodical, Fielding directly challenged the "armies of Grub Street" and the other periodical writers of the day in a conflict that would eventually become the Paper War of 1752–3.

Fielding then published, in 1753, "Examples of the interposition of Providence in the Detection and Punishment of Murder, a work in which, rejecting the deistic and materialistic visions of the world, he wrote in favour of the belief in God's presence and divine judgement, arguing that the rise of murder rates was due to neglect of the Christian religion. In 1753 he would add to this with Proposals for making an effectual Provision for the Poor.

Fielding's ardent commitment to the cause of justice as a great humanitarian in the 1750s unfortunately coincided with a rapid deterioration in his health. Such was his decline that in the summer of 1754 he travelled, with Mary and his daughter, to Portugal in search of a cure. Gout, asthma, dropsy and other afflictions forced him to use crutches. His health continued to fail alarmingly.

Henry Fielding died in Lisbon two months later on October 8th, 1754.

His tomb is in the city's English Cemetery (Cemitério Inglês), which is now the graveyard of St. George's Church, Lisbon.

Henry Fielding – A Concise Bibliography

The Masquerade, a poem
Love in Several Masques, a play, 1728
Rape Upon Rape, a play, 1730.
The Temple Beau, a play, 1730
The Author's Farce, a play, 1730
The Letter Writers, a play, 1731

The Tragedy of Tragedies; or, The Life and Death of Tom Thumb the Great, a play, 1731
Grub-Street Opera, a play, 1731
The Roast Beef of Old England, 1731
The Modern Husband, a play, 1732
The Mock Doctor, a play, 1732
The Lottery, a play, 1732
The Covent Garden Tragedy, a play, 1732
The Miser, a play, 1732
The Old Debauchees, a play 1732
The Intriguing Chambermaid, a play, 1734
Don Quixote in England, a play, 1734
Pasquin, a play, 1736
Eurydice Hiss'd, a play, 1737
The Historical Register for the Year 1736, a play, 1737
An Apology for the Life of Mrs. Shamela Andrews, a novel, 1741
The History of the Adventures of Joseph Andrews & his Friend, Mr. Abraham Abrams, a novel, 1742
The Life and Death of Jonathan Wild, the Great, a novel, 1743.
Miscellanies – collection of works, 1743, contained the poem Part of Juvenal's Sixth Satire, Modernized in Burlesque Verse
The Female Husband or the Surprising History of Mrs Mary alias Mr George Hamilton, who was convicted of having married a young woman of Wells and lived with her as her husband, taken from her own mouth since her confinement, a pamphlet, fictionalized report, 1746
The History of Tom Jones, a Foundling, a novel, 1749
A Journey from this World to the Next – 1749
Amelia, a novel, 1751
"Examples of the interposition of Providence in the Detection and Punishment of Murder containing above thirty cases in which this dreadful crime has been brought to light in the most extraordinary and miraculous manner; collected from various authors, ancient and modern", 1752
The Covent Garden Journal, a periodical, 1752
Journal of a Voyage to Lisbon, a travel narrative, 1755
The Fathers: Or, the Good-Natur'd Man, a play, published posthumously in 1778

Other Works (Undated)
An Old Man or The Virgin Unmasked
Miss Lucy in Town, a Play, a sequel to The Virgin Unmasked
Plutus with William Young from the Greek play by Aristophanes.
The Temple Beau, a play
The Wedding Beau, a play
The Welsh Opera
Tumble-Down Dick
An Essay on Conversation, an Essay
The True Patriot, a letter